Collins

Reading

KS1 English Reading

SATs Question Book

Age 6–7

Key Stage 1

SATs Question Book

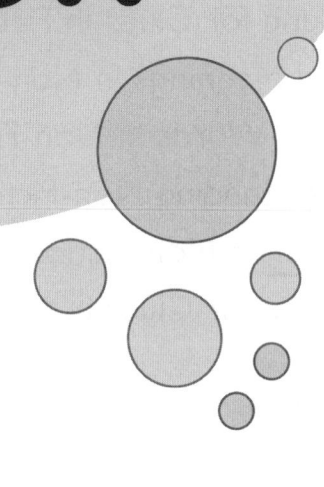

Alison Head

Contents

Preparing for Paper 1

Word Meanings in Poems 4
Finding Words in Poems 6
Understanding Poetry 8
Finding Information in Non-Fiction 10
Explaining Non-Fiction 12
Finding Information in Fiction 14
Explaining Fiction 16
Putting Events in Order 18
Predicting What Will Happen 19
Looking for Clues in Fiction 20

Progress Test 1 24

Preparing for Paper 2

Word Meanings in Fiction 28
Finding Words in Fiction 29
Understanding Fiction 30
Explaining Fiction 32
Putting Events in Order 34
Predicting What Will Happen 35
Looking for Clues in Fiction 36
Word Meanings in Non-Fiction 38
Finding Words in Non-Fiction 39
Understanding Non-Fiction 40
Explaining Non-Fiction 42
Looking for Clues in Non-Fiction 44

Progress Test 2 46

Answers and Progress Test Charts 49

Reading Booklet (Pull-out) 1-8

How to Use this Book

- You will need a pen or pencil and a rubber.

- The first part of this book focuses on Reading Paper 1. The texts are broken down into short sections and are followed by questions that focus on that section.

- The second part of the book focuses on Reading Paper 2. You will need to use the pull-out reading booklet in the centre of this book to answer the questions. The page numbers given in brackets next to the questions tell you what page of the reading booklet you need to look at to find the answer.

- There are different types of question for you to answer in different ways. The space for your answer shows you what type of answer is needed.

- Some questions are multiple choice, some are short answers where you need only write a word or a few words, and others are longer and followed by several lines to give you space to write more words or a sentence or two.

- Always read the instructions carefully so that you know how to answer each question.

- The number of marks for each question will help you to know how much detail you need to give in your answer.

- There are two progress tests to allow you to practise the skills again. Record your results in the progress charts to identify what you are doing well in and what you can improve.

Useful Words
Page 12   axle: a rod joining two wheels

Page 13   spokes: the bars on a wheel that join the outer ring to the centre

Page 21   somersaults: someone or something turning over in the air

Page 21   Catherine-wheel: a type of firework that spins very fast

Preparing for Paper 1

Word Meanings in Poems

Daddy Fell into the Pond

Everyone grumbled. The sky was grey.
We had nothing to do and nothing to say.
We were nearing the end of a dismal day,
And there seemed to be nothing beyond,
Then
Daddy fell into the pond!

And everyone's face grew merry and bright,
And Timothy danced for sheer delight.
"Give me the camera, quick, oh quick!
He's crawling out of the duckweed!"
Click!

Then the gardener suddenly slapped his knee,
And doubled up, shaking silently,
And the ducks all quacked as if they were daft,
And it sounded as if the old drake laughed.
Oh, there wasn't a thing that didn't respond
When
Daddy fell into the pond!

---

1 *Everyone grumbled.*

What does this mean?

Tick one.

Everyone argued. ☐

Everyone complained. ☐

Everyone cried. ☐

Everyone laughed. ☐

1 mark

Preparing for Paper 1

Word Meanings in Poems

2 The day was *dismal*.

This means that it was...

Tick one.

rainy. ☐

boring. ☐

gloomy. ☐

cold. ☐

1 mark

3 *Timothy danced for sheer delight.*

What does this mean?

Tick one.

Timothy danced beautifully. ☐

Timothy danced because he was happy. ☐

Timothy danced because he was bored. ☐

Timothy danced to cheer himself up. ☐

1 mark

Total marks ..../3   How am I doing?

Preparing for Paper 1

Finding Words in Poems

Daddy Fell into the Pond

Everyone grumbled. The sky was grey.
We had nothing to do and nothing to say.
We were nearing the end of a dismal day,
And there seemed to be nothing beyond,
Then
Daddy fell into the pond!

And everyone's face grew merry and bright,
And Timothy danced for sheer delight.
"Give me the camera, quick, oh quick!
He's crawling out of the duckweed!"
Click!

Then the gardener suddenly slapped his knee,
And doubled up, shaking silently,
And the ducks all quacked as if they were daft,
And it sounded as if the old drake laughed.
Oh, there wasn't a thing that didn't respond
When
Daddy fell into the pond!

Preparing for Paper 1

Finding Words in Poems

1 **Find** and **copy one** word that shows that Daddy came out of the pond on his hands and knees.

_____

1 mark

2 **Find** and **copy one** word that shows that the gardener did not make a sound when he was laughing.

_____

1 mark

3 **Find** and **copy one** word that means *male duck*.

_____

1 mark

4 **Find** and **copy one** word that means *react*.

_____

1 mark

Total marks .... /4   How am I doing?

Preparing for Paper 1

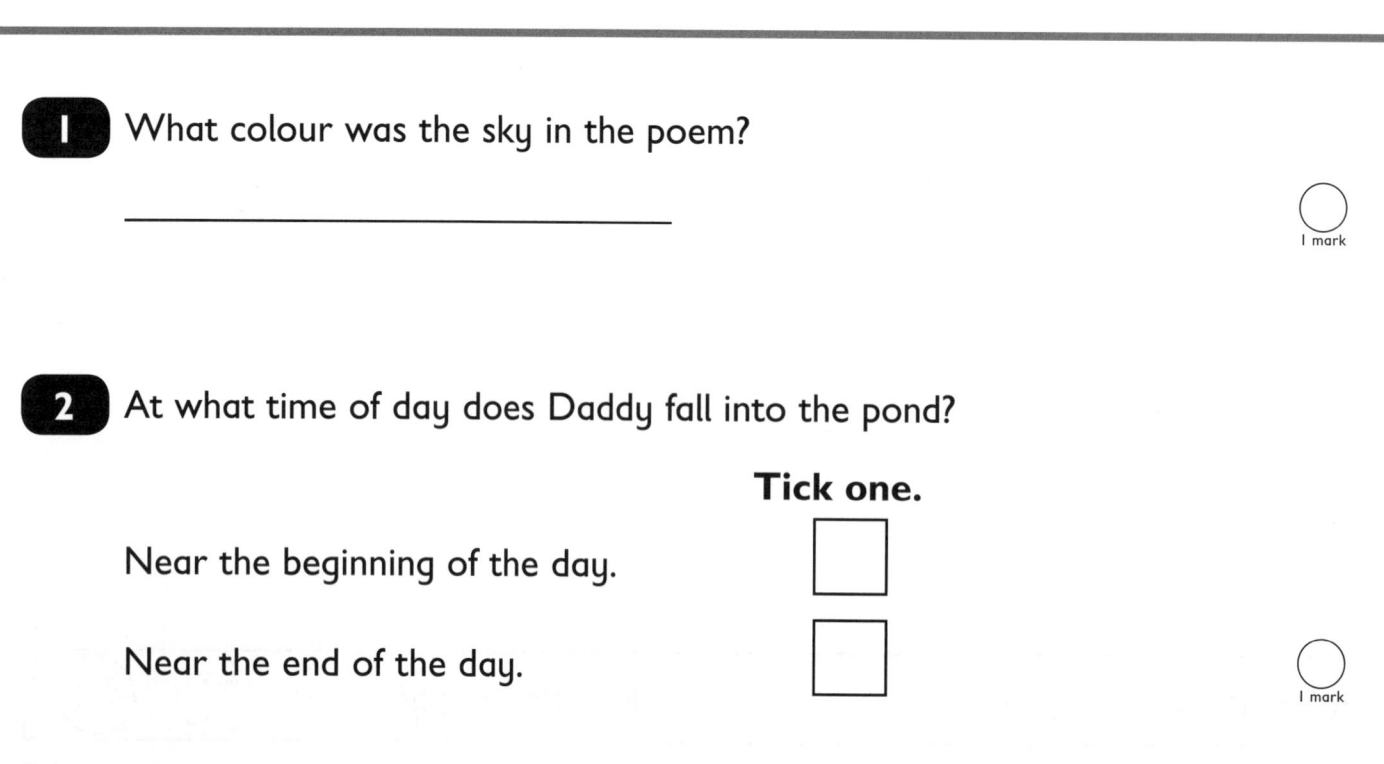

Understanding Poetry

Daddy Fell into the Pond

Everyone grumbled. The sky was grey.
We had nothing to do and nothing to say.
We were nearing the end of a dismal day,
And there seemed to be nothing beyond,
Then
Daddy fell into the pond!

And everyone's face grew merry and bright,
And Timothy danced for sheer delight.
"Give me the camera, quick, oh quick!
He's crawling out of the duckweed!"
Click!

Then the gardener suddenly slapped his knee,
And doubled up, shaking silently,
And the ducks all quacked as if they were daft,
And it sounded as if the old drake laughed.
Oh, there wasn't a thing that didn't respond
When
Daddy fell into the pond!

---

1 What colour was the sky in the poem?

_____

1 mark

2 At what time of day does Daddy fall into the pond?

Tick one.

Near the beginning of the day. ☐

Near the end of the day. ☐

1 mark

Preparing for Paper 1

Understanding Poetry

3 What makes a *click* sound?

Tick one.

a duck ☐

Daddy falling in the pond ☐

the gardener slapping his knee ☐

the camera ☐

1 mark

4 Who or what made a noise that sounded like laughing?

Tick one.

the gardener ☐

the old drake ☐

Timothy ☐

Daddy ☐

1 mark

Total marks .... /4   How am I doing?

9

Preparing for Paper 1

Finding Information in Non-Fiction

Inventing the Wheel

Imagine life without wheels. With no cars, trains, bikes or buses — or even wheelbarrows — getting around would be miserably slow. Luckily, wheels were invented a long, long time ago.

Wheel-free world
6,000 years ago, no one had wheels. But it didn't matter so much because, in those days, there were hardly any roads. Many people lived in forests, deserts or boggy swamps, where wheels wouldn't have been much use. They walked everywhere, and used animals to carry heavy loads.

1 Where did many people used to live 6,000 years ago?

_____

1 mark

2 Why didn't it matter that there were not many roads 6,000 years ago?

_____

1 mark

3 Tick to show what people and animals did before wheels were invented.

	People	Animals
carried heavy loads		
walked everywhere		

1 mark

Preparing for Paper 1

Finding Information in Non-Fiction

Did you know?
Nobody knows exactly where or when the first wheel was invented, but the earliest pictures of wheels are around 5,200 years old, and come from Sumeria (an ancient civilization in what is now Iraq). They show carts with solid, wooden wheels made from planks, pulled by onagers (a type of wild donkey). It would have been a bumpy ride, but wheels helped the Sumerians to travel faster and carry loads much more easily than before.

4 What is an *onager*?

Tick one.

a solid, wooden wheel ☐

a wild donkey ☐

a cart ☐

a plank ☐

1 mark

5 In which modern country was Sumeria once found?

_____

1 mark

6 What were early wheels made from?

_____

1 mark

Total marks ………… /6   How am I doing?

11

Preparing for Paper 1

Explaining Non-Fiction

Inventing the Wheel

Wheels of progress

Most experts think wheels developed slowly over many, many years. They probably weren't invented by a single person.

Before wheels, people often dragged things along using ropes. Then they found that putting logs under a heavy load made it roll and move more easily.

A sledge mounted on logs made a good transporter. The sides of the sledge wore grooves in the logs. The next step was to cut away the inner part of the log to make an axle. The ends worked like wheels.

1 Before wheels, how did people use rope to move things?

_____

1 mark

2 How did putting logs under a heavy load help people to move heavy loads?

_____

1 mark

3 What did the ends of the axle work like?

_____

1 mark

Preparing for Paper 1

Explaining Non-Fiction

From wooden wheels to tyres

Over time people learned to fix the axle to a sledge or cart so that the wheels could spin around freely.

Solid wooden wheels were very heavy, so the next step was to invent spokes. The first people to do this lived 4,000 years ago in central Asia.

Pneumatic (air-filled) tyres were first invented in 1845 by Scottish inventor Robert Thomson. Used on carriages and bicycles, they made for a much smoother ride.

4 What was the problem with solid wooden wheels?

_____

1 mark

5 Why did people invent spokes?

_____

1 mark

6 How were air-filled tyres better than solid wheels?

_____

1 mark

Total marks ………… /6   How am I doing?

Preparing for Paper 1

Finding Information in Fiction

The Owl Who Was Afraid of the Dark

Plop was a baby barn owl, and he lived with his mummy and daddy at the top of a very tall tree in a field.

Plop was fat and fluffy.

He had a beautiful heart-shaped ruff.

He had enormous, round eyes.

He had very knackety knees.

In fact he was exactly the same as every baby barn owl that has ever been – except for one thing.

Plop was afraid of the dark.

---

1 Where is the tree that Plop lives in?
_____

1 mark

2 What shape is Plop's ruff?
_____

1 mark

3 How was Plop different from other baby barn owls?

Tick one.

He was fat. ☐

He was fluffy. ☐

He was afraid of the dark. ☐

His eyes were round. ☐

1 mark

Preparing for Paper 1

Finding Information in Fiction

'You *can't* be afraid of the dark', said his mummy. 'Owls are *never* afraid of the dark.'

'This one is,' Plop said.

'But owls are *night* birds,' she said.

Plop looked down at his toes. 'I don't want to be a night bird,' he mumbled. 'I want to be a day bird.'

'You *are* what you *are*,' said Mrs Barn Owl firmly.

'Yes, I know,' agreed Plop, 'and what I are is afraid of the dark.'

---

4 Who tells Plop that owls are never afraid of the dark?

_____

1 mark

5 Night birds and day birds are mentioned in the story.

Which type of bird does Plop **not** want to be and which does he want to be?

Plop does **not** want to be a _____ bird.

Plop wants to be a _____ bird.

1 mark

6 Does what Mrs Barn Owl says to Plop change his mind about being afraid?

Tick one.

yes ☐

no ☐

1 mark

Total marks .... /6   How am I doing?

15

Preparing for Paper 1

Explaining Fiction

The Owl Who Was Afraid of the Dark

'Oh dear,' said Mrs Barn Owl. It was clear that she was going to need a lot of patience. She shut her eyes and tried to think how best she could help Plop not to be afraid. Plop waited.

His mother opened her eyes again. 'Plop, you are only afraid of the dark because you don't know about it. What do you know about the dark?'

'It's black,' said Plop.

'Well, that's wrong for a start. It can be silver or blue or grey or lots of other colours, but almost never black. What else do you know about it?'

1 What does Mrs Barn Owl want to help Plop to do?

_____

1 mark

2 Why does Mrs Barn Owl think Plop is afraid of the dark?

_____

1 mark

3 Give **two** colours that Mrs Barn Owl says the night can be.

1. _____

2. _____

1 mark

Preparing for Paper 1

Explaining Fiction

'I don't like it,' said Plop. 'I do not like it AT ALL.'

'That's not *knowing* something,' said his mother. That's *feeling* something. I don't think you know anything about the dark at all.

'Dark is nasty,' Plop said loudly.

'You don't know that. You have never had your beak outside the nest-hole after dark. I think you had better go down into the world and find out a lot more about the dark before you make up your mind about it.

'Now?' said Plop.

'Now,' said his mother.

---

4 Why does Mrs Barn Owl say that Plop does not know that dark is nasty?

_____

_____
1 mark

5 Where does Mrs Barn Owl tell Plop he should go to find out more about the dark?

_____
1 mark

6 When does she think he should go?

_____
1 mark

Total marks ………… /6   How am I doing?

Preparing for Paper 1

Putting Events in Order

1 On page 14 we find out a lot about Plop.

Number the sentences from 1 to 4 to show the order we find out information about him.

The first one has been done for you.

Plop was afraid of the dark. ☐

Plop was fat and fluffy. ☐

Plop had knackety knees. ☐

Plop lived with his mummy and daddy. [1]

1 mark

2 Number the sentences from 1 to 4 to show the order they happened in the story.

The first one has been done for you.

Plop's mummy wants to help him not to be afraid. ☐

Plop tells his mummy he is afraid of the dark. [1]

Plop's mummy tells him to go down into the world. ☐

Plop's mummy tells him he does not know enough about the dark. ☐

1 mark

Total marks .... /2   How am I doing?

Preparing for Paper 1

Predicting What Will Happen

1 What do you think will happen next in the story?

Tick one.

Plop will turn into a day bird. ☐

Plop will go down into the world during the day time. ☐

Plop will go to live in a zoo. ☐

Plop will go to live in a different tree. ☐

1 mark

2 Explain how you think Plop would feel before going down into the world.

_____

_____

_____

1 mark

Total marks ………… /2   How am I doing?

Preparing for Paper 1

Looking for Clues in Fiction

The Owl Who Was Afraid of the Dark

Plop climbed out of the nest-hole and wobbled along the branch outside. He peeped over the edge. The world seemed to be a very long way down.

'I'm not a very good lander,' he said. 'I might spill myself.'

'Your landing will improve with practice,' said his mother. 'Look! There's a little boy down there on the edge of the wood collecting sticks. Go and talk to him about it.'

'Now?' said Plop.

'Now,' said his mother. So Plop shut his eyes, took a deep breath, and fell off the branch.

---

1 Why did Plop think the world seemed to be a very long way down?

_____

1 mark

2 What do you think Plop means when he says he might 'spill' himself?

_____

1 mark

3 Give **two** things that Plop does just before he falls off the branch that tell you he is nervous.

1. _____

2. _____

1 mark

Looking for Clues in Fiction

Preparing for Paper 1

His small white wings carried him down, but, as he said, he was not a good lander. He did seven very fast somersaults past the little boy.

'Ooh!' cried the little boy. 'A giant Catherine-wheel!'

'Actually,' said the Catherine-wheel, picking himself up, 'I'm a barn owl.'

'Oh yes – so you are,' said the little boy with obvious disappointment. 'Of course, you couldn't be a firework yet. Dad says we can't have the fireworks until it gets dark. Oh, I wish it would hurry up and get dark soon.'

4 How is Plop like a Catherine-wheel firework when he lands?

_____

_____

1 mark

5 Why is the boy disappointed when he finds out that Plop is not a firework?

_____

_____

1 mark

6 Why does the little boy want it to 'hurry up and get dark soon'?

_____

_____

1 mark

Preparing for Paper 1

Looking for Clues in Fiction

'You want it to get dark?' said Plop in amazement.

'Oh YES,' said the little boy. 'DARK IS EXCITING. And tonight is specially exciting because we're going to have fireworks.'

'What are fireworks?' asked Plop. 'I don't think owls have them – not barn owls anyway.'

'Don't you?' said the little boy. 'Oh you poor thing. Well, there are rockets, and flying saucers, and volcanoes, and golden rain, and sparklers, and…'

'But what *are* they?' begged Plop. 'Do you eat them?'

'NO!' laughed the little boy. 'Daddy sets fire to their tails and they whoosh into the air and fill the sky with coloured stars – well the rockets, that is. I'm allowed to hold the sparklers.'

---

7 **Find** and **copy one** word that shows how surprised Plop is that the little boy wants it to get dark.

_____

1 mark

8 Why does the little boy say, 'Oh you poor thing' when Plop tells him that owls do not have fireworks?

_____

_____

1 mark

9 The little boy thinks it is funny that Plop does not know what a firework is. How do you know that the boy thinks it is funny?

_____

1 mark

Preparing for Paper 1

Looking for Clues in Fiction

'What about the volcanoes? And the golden rain? What do they do?'

'Oh, they sort of burst into showers of stars. The golden rain pours – well, like rain.'

'And the flying saucers?'

'Oh, they're super! They whizz round your head and make a sort of wheeee noise. I like them best.'

'I think I would like fireworks,' said Plop.

'I'm sure you would,' the little boy said. 'Look here, where do you live?'

'Up in that tree – in the top flat. There are squirrels farther down.'

'That big tree in the middle of the field? Well, you can watch our fireworks from there!'

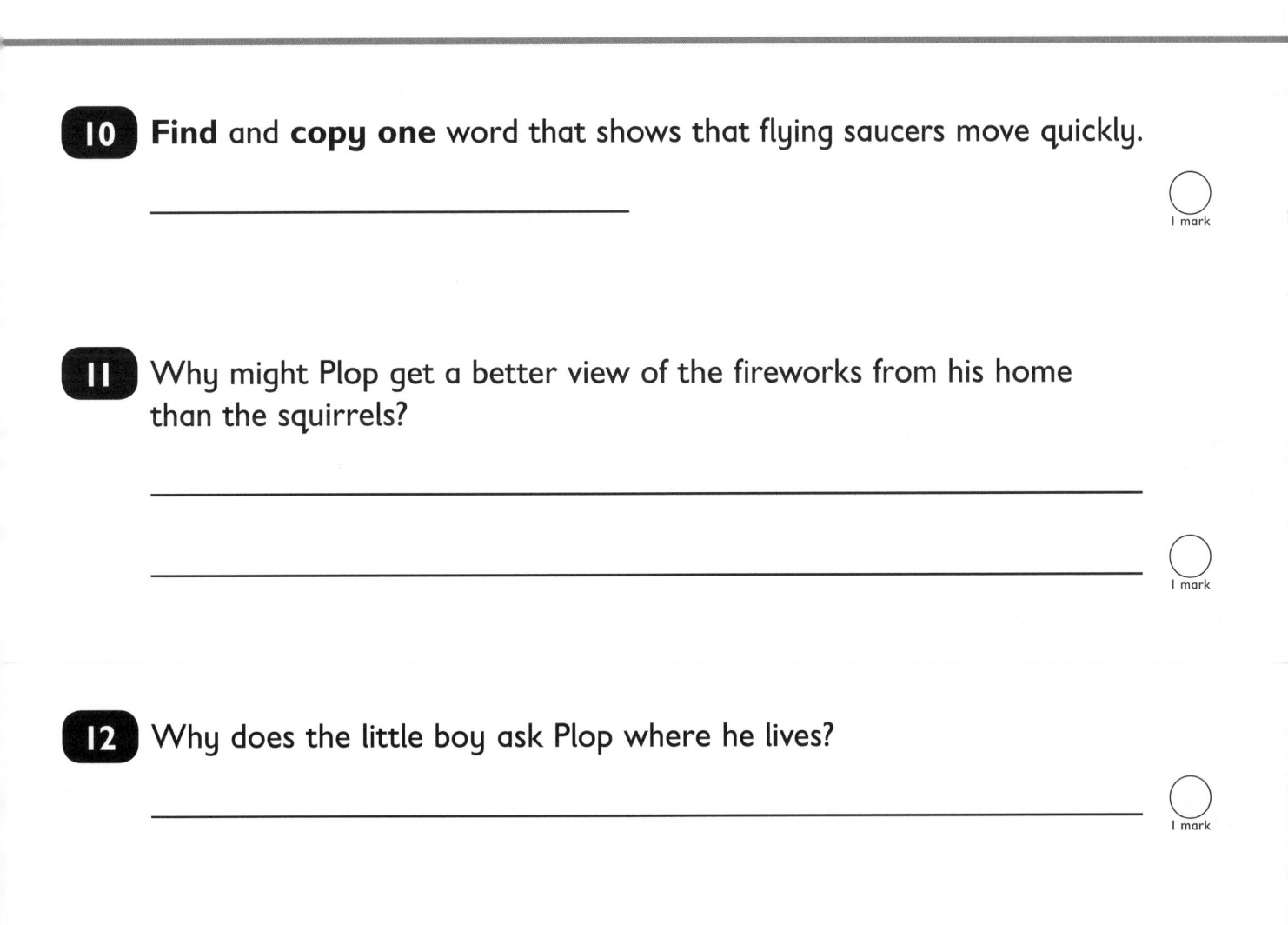

---

10 **Find** and **copy one** word that shows that flying saucers move quickly.

_____

1 mark

11 Why might Plop get a better view of the fireworks from his home than the squirrels?

_____

_____

1 mark

12 Why does the little boy ask Plop where he lives?

_____

1 mark

Total marks .... /12   How am I doing?

Preparing for Paper 1

Progress Test 1

Little White Lily

Little White Lily
Sat by a stone,
Drooping and waiting
Till the sun shone.
Little White Lily
Sunshine has fed;
Little White Lily
Is lifting her head.

1 What is the *Little White Lily*? **Tick one.**

a girl ☐   a flower ☐

a cloud ☐   a river ☐

1 mark

2 **Find** and **copy one** word that means *wilting*.

_____

1 mark

3 Where is the lily?

_____

1 mark

4 What is the lily waiting for?

_____

1 mark

Preparing for Paper 1

Progress Test 1

Esio Trot

Mr Hoppy lived in a small flat high up in a tall concrete building. He lived alone. He had always been a lonely man and now that he was retired from work he was more lonely than ever.

There were two loves in Mr Hoppy's life. One was the flowers he grew on his balcony. They grew in pots and tubs and baskets, and in summer the little balcony was a riot of colour.

5 What is the building Mr Hoppy lives in made from?

_____

1 mark

6 Does Mr Hoppy have a job?

_____

1 mark

7 *the little balcony was a riot of colour*

What does this mean?

Tick one.

The balcony was noisy. ☐

The balcony was painted in bright colours. ☐

The balcony was filled with colourful flowers. ☐

Mr Hoppy loved his balcony. ☐

1 mark

25

Preparing for Paper 1

Progress Test 1

The Hedgehog

The hedgehog is an easy animal to identify. It is covered in a thick coat of spines. When a hedgehog is attacked by another animal, it curls up into a tight ball with all its spines sticking out.

The hedgehog is a small grey-brown animal, with a long nose and round, bead-like eyes. Male and female hedgehogs look very similar. Their babies are called hoglets.

8 What is a hedgehog's body covered in?

_____

1 mark

9 How do hedgehogs defend themselves?

_____

1 mark

10 Put ticks in the table to show which sentences are **true** and which sentences are **false**.

Sentence	True	False
Hedgehogs are black.		
Male and female hedgehogs look very different.		
Hedgehogs have long noses.		
Baby hedgehogs are called hoglets.		

2 marks

26

Preparing for Paper 1

Progress Test 1

Animal FACTS

- An adult hedgehog is between 20 and 30 cm in length.
- It weighs between 1 and 2 kg.
- Hedgehogs live for two to three years, sometimes as long as five years.
- Hedgehogs are nocturnal; they are active at night.
- The Latin name for hedgehogs is *Erinaceus europaeus*.

11 What does the heading *Animal FACTS* tell you about the information?

Tick one.

It is true. ☐

It is not true. ☐

1 mark

12 How long can an adult hedgehog be?

_____

1 mark

13 Why are hedgehogs active at night?

_____

1 mark

14 How long can hedgehogs sometimes live for?

_____

1 mark

Total marks ………… /15   How am I doing?

Preparing for Paper 2

Word Meanings in Fiction

Use the pull-out Reading booklet to answer the questions in this half of the book.

These questions are about *The Monkey's Heart.*

1 The crocodile *basked* in the sun. (Page 3)

What does this mean?

Tick one.

He waited in the sun. ☐

He lay in the sun. ☐

He ran about in the sun. ☐

He wriggled in the sun. ☐

1 mark

2 *He wasn't the brightest of creatures.* (Page 4)

What does this mean?

Tick one.

The crocodile was a dull green colour. ☐

The crocodile swam slowly. ☐

The crocodile was not shiny. ☐

The crocodile was not very clever. ☐

1 mark

Total marks .... /2   How am I doing?

The Monkey's Heart

The Great Fire of London

Reading Booklet

Key Stage 1 English Reading Booklet

Contents

The Monkey's Heart — Pages 3–5

The Great Fire of London — Pages 6–7

The Monkey's Heart

"All we ever eat is fish, fish and more fish," complained the crocodile's wife. "Wouldn't it be nice to have a change?"

"I've never really thought about it," the crocodile yawned as he basked in the hot sun.

"There's a little monkey that lives on the riverbank," said his wife. "It eats nothing but mangoes all day long. I bet its heart tastes deliciously sweet. Go and catch it – we'll eat it for dinner."

"It's too hot to be rushing around catching monkeys," the crocodile murmured.

"Too hot?" snapped his wife. "You mean you can't be bothered! Don't you even love me enough to feed me one tiny monkey's heart?" she sniffed, and two big crocodile tears rolled slowly down her face.

"All right, I'll see what I can do," sighed the crocodile, and he slipped into the river. He floated in the cool water, trying to think of a plan to catch the monkey. He wasn't the brightest of creatures, so it took him all afternoon.

As the sun was beginning to set, the crocodile swam over to the far riverbank, where the monkey was sitting in a mango tree.

"Hello up there!" he called to the monkey.

"Hello!" the monkey called back.

The crocodile smiled his largest, most inviting smile. "My wife and I," he said, "were thinking how nice it would be to have you for dinner – er, I mean – to have you over for dinner. We see you near the river so often and it would be good to get to know you better."

"That's very kind," said the monkey. "I'd love to come."

"We live on the other side," said the crocodile. "I can take you there on my back, if you like."

"Thank you very much," said the monkey, and he ran down the tree and hopped onto the crocodile's back.

When they were halfway across the river, the crocodile began to rock from side to side.

"Hey!" shouted the monkey, in alarm. "What are you doing?"

"Ha!" jeered the crocodile. "Did you really think I wanted to be your friend? It was a trick! Now my wife and I are going to eat your heart for dinner."

"Oh dear," said the monkey, shaking his head. "What a shame. You should have told me before we set off."

"What do you mean?" asked the crocodile.

"Didn't you know?" said the monkey. "Monkeys don't wear their hearts all the time. We only use them on special occasions. If you'd told me, I'd have brought it with me."

"Oh," said the crocodile, looking terribly disappointed. "I don't suppose we could go back and get it?"

"Of course," said the monkey. "It's hanging over there on that tree," and he pointed to a fig tree on the riverbank. The crocodile swam, over to the tree, his mouth watering at the thought of the monkey's sweet heart.

As soon as they reached the bank, the monkey leaped off the crocodile's back and scampered up into the branches. Once he was safely out of reach, he stopped and looked back.

"You fish-brain!" he laughed.

"Did you really think that monkeys keep their hearts in the treetops? So much for making friends with a crocodile. I'll never trust you again!"

So the crocodile and his wife never did get to taste a monkey's heart. For the rest of their days, they had to make do with fish – for breakfast, lunch and dinner.

The Great Fire of London

The summer of 1666 was hot and dry in London. The streets were narrow and crammed with tall wooden houses on each side. The streets were dirty and filled with rubbish.

Late at night on Saturday 1st September, a baker in Pudding Lane checked the fires in his ovens and then went to bed. In the middle of the night he woke to the smell of smoke and realised his house was on fire!

The fire spread rapidly to nearby houses and sparks floated into the air, setting fire to rubbish in the street. Some sparks landed on warehouses by the river. The warehouses were full of flammable goods that burn easily, like oil and brandy. This made the fire much worse. A strong east wind fanned the flames and helped the fire spread quickly.

The Mayor of London was not worried. He thought the fire would be easy to put out but by the morning, hundreds of houses had burned to the ground. King Charles II took control. He told the people to pull down some houses so that the fire would have nothing to burn, but this did not work. The flames were too big and they jumped over the gap.

Tuesday 4th September was the worst day of the fire. Even St Paul's Cathedral, which was made of stone, was destroyed. The flames were so fierce that the lead metal on its roof melted and ran through the streets.

Finally, the wind changed direction and the fire died down. Much of London was in ruins and many thousands of people had lost their homes.

King Charles wanted to rebuild the city even better than before and he asked a man called Christopher Wren to design the new city. King Charles loved the designs, but he could not afford to build everything in the plan.

It took years to rebuild the city. Lots of new rules were made to try to make sure there would never be another big fire. All new buildings had to be built from brick or stone because wood burned too easily. Fire brigades were set up and people were instructed to clear away their rubbish and check their fires carefully at night.

Today you can still visit the new St Paul's Cathedral designed by Wren, with its famous domed roof.

Preparing for Paper 2

Finding Words in Fiction

These questions are about *The Monkey's Heart*.

1 **Find** and **copy one** word from the first line of the story that means *grumbled*. (Page 3)

_____

1 mark

2 **Find** and **copy one** word that shows that the crocodile felt sleepy as he lay in the sun. (Page 3)

_____

1 mark

3 **Find** and **copy one** word that means *hurrying*. (Page 3)

_____

1 mark

4 **Find** and **copy one** word that means *scheme*. (Page 4)

_____

1 mark

5 **Find** and **copy one** word that means *mocked*. (Page 5)

_____

1 mark

Total marks .... /5   How am I doing?

Preparing for Paper 2

Understanding Fiction

These questions are about *The Monkey's Heart.*

1 What does the crocodile's wife say the monkey eats all day? (Page 3)

Tick one.

figs ☐

dinner ☐

fish ☐

mangoes ☐

1 mark

2 What is the first thing the crocodile does after he slides into the river? (Page 4)

Tick one.

He floats in the water. ☐

He swims across the river. ☐

He basks in the sunshine. ☐

He rocks from side to side. ☐

1 mark

3 Put ticks in the table to show which sentences are **true** and which sentences are **false**. (Pages 3–4)

Sentence	True	False
The crocodile and his wife eat a lot of fish.		
The weather in the story is hot.		
The monkey was sitting in a fig tree.		
The crocodile tells the monkey a joke.		

2 marks

Preparing for Paper 2

Understanding Fiction

4 Put ticks in the table to show which sentences are **true** and which sentences are **false**.

(Pages 4–5)

Sentence	True	False
The monkey agrees to go for dinner with the crocodiles.		
The monkey swims across the river.		
The monkey escapes into a tree.		
The monkey calls the crocodile 'fish-face'.		

2 marks

5 The crocodile and the monkey both play a trick. (Pages 4–5)

Which trick does each one play?

Trick	Animal
Pretends to be a friend but plans to eat him.	
Pretends he does not have his heart with him.	

1 mark

6 Where does the monkey say his heart is? (Page 5)

Tick one.

in a mango tree ☐

in his chest ☐

on the riverbank ☐

in a fig tree ☐

1 mark

Total marks .... /8   How am I doing? 😊 😐 ☹

Preparing for Paper 2

Explaining Fiction

These questions are about *The Monkey's Heart*.

1 Why does the crocodile say he doesn't want to catch the monkey? (Page 3)

_____

_____
1 mark

2 Why does he change his mind? (Page 4)

_____

_____
1 mark

3 What part of the monkey does the crocodile's wife want to eat? (Page 4)

_____
1 mark

4 How long does it take the crocodile to think of a plan? (Page 4)

_____
1 mark

5 What reason does the crocodile give for inviting the monkey over for dinner? (Page 4)

_____

_____
1 mark

32

Preparing for Paper 2

Explaining Fiction

6 How does the crocodile suggest the monkey could cross the river? (Page 4)

_____ 1 mark

7 When does the monkey say he uses his heart? (Page 5)

_____ 1 mark

8 Why is the crocodile's mouth watering? (Page 5)

_____
_____ 1 mark

9 Why does the crocodile look 'terribly disappointed'? (Page 5)

_____
_____ 1 mark

10 What did the monkey do when he was safely out of reach of the crocodile? (Page 5)

_____
_____ 1 mark

Total marks ………… /10   How am I doing?

Preparing for Paper 2

Putting Events in Order

This question is about *The Monkey's Heart*.

1 Number the sentences from 1 to 4 to show the order they happened in the story.

(Pages 3–5)

The first one has been done for you.

The crocodile swims across to the far riverbank. ☐

The crocodile's wife says she is tired of eating fish. 1

The crocodile thinks of a plan to catch the monkey. ☐

The crocodile's wife asks him to catch the monkey. ☐

1 mark

This question is about *The Great Fire of London*.

2 Number the sentences from 1 to 4 to show the order they happened in the text.

(Pages 6–7)

The first one has been done for you.

St Paul's Cathedral was destroyed. ☐

The warehouses caught fire. 1

Christopher Wren designed a new city. ☐

King Charles II told people to pull down houses to try and stop the fire. ☐

1 mark

Total marks .... /2   How am I doing? ☺ ☺ ☹

Preparing for Paper 2

Predicting What Will Happen

This question is about *The Monkey's Heart*.

1 What do you think the crocodile's wife will do when she finds out what has happened? (Pages 3–5)

Tick one.

She will eat a mango. ☐

She will be very angry with the crocodile. ☐

She will be very pleased with the crocodile. ☐

She will bake a pie for dinner. ☐

1 mark

2 Do you think the monkey will ever trust a crocodile again? (Pages 3–5)

Give a reason for your answer.

_____

_____

_____

2 marks

Total marks .... /3   How am I doing?

Preparing for Paper 2

Looking for Clues in Fiction

> These questions are about *The Monkey's Heart.*

1 Why do you think the crocodile's wife *snapped* at him? (Pages 3–4)

_____

_____

1 mark

2 Why did the crocodile smile his widest, most inviting smile? (Page 4)

_____

_____

1 mark

3 **Find** and **copy one** word that shows that the crocodile does not really want to try to catch the monkey at first. (Page 4)

_____

1 mark

4 Is the monkey afraid when the crocodile tells him he is going to eat him? (Pages 4–5)

Give a reason for your answer.

_____

_____

_____

1 mark

36

Preparing for Paper 2

Looking for Clues in Fiction

5 Why does the crocodile's plan to catch the monkey fail? (Pages 4–5)

_____
_____
_____

○ 1 mark

6 Why does the monkey tell the crocodile he keeps his heart in a fig tree? (Page 5)

_____
_____
_____

○ 1 mark

7 Why does the monkey call the crocodile "*You fish-brain!*"? (Page 5)

_____
_____

○ 1 mark

8 Do you think the monkey can swim? (Pages 4–5)

Give a reason for your answer.

_____
_____
_____

○ 1 mark

Total marks .... /8   How am I doing? 😊 😐 😣

37

Preparing for Paper 2

Word Meanings in Non-Fiction

> These questions are about *The Great Fire of London.*

1 The fire spread *rapidly*. (Page 6)

This means that the fire spread…

Tick one.

slowly. ☐

quickly. ☐

silently. ☐

luckily. ☐

1 mark

2 The flames were *fierce*. (Pages 6–7)

This means that the flames were…

Tick one.

noisy. ☐

powerful. ☐

angry. ☐

sharp. ☐

1 mark

Total marks ………… /2   How am I doing?

Preparing for Paper 2

Finding Words in Non-Fiction

These questions are about *The Great Fire of London*.

1 **Find** and **copy one** word from the start of the text that shows that the streets were not wide. (Page 6)

_____

1 mark

2 **Find** and **copy one** word from the start of the text that shows that the streets are packed with houses. (Page 6)

_____

1 mark

3 **Find** and **copy one** word from paragraph 3 that means *products*. (Page 6)

_____

1 mark

4 **Find** and **copy one** word from paragraph 5 that means *roads*. (Page 7)

_____

1 mark

5 **Find** and **copy one** word from paragraph 6 than means *in the end*. (Page 7)

_____

1 mark

Total marks .... /5   How am I doing?

Preparing for Paper 2

Understanding Non-Fiction

> These questions are about *The Great Fire of London.*

1 On what day of the week was the worst day of the fire? (Page 6)

Tick one.

Saturday ☐

Tuesday ☐

Monday ☐

Friday ☐

1 mark

2 Who tried to stop the fire by telling people to pull down houses? (Page 6)

Tick one.

Christopher Wren ☐

Mayor of London ☐

King Charles II ☐

a baker in Pudding Lane ☐

1 mark

3 Tick to show how London was different before and after the Great Fire. (Pages 6–7)

	Before the Fire	After the Fire
Rubbish in the streets		
New buildings built of brick or stone		
Houses made of wood		
Fire brigades set up		

2 marks

Preparing for Paper 2

Understanding Non-Fiction

4 Put ticks in the table to show which statements are **true** and which statements are **false**. (Pages 6–7)

Statement	True	False
The summer of 1666 was hot in London.		
The Great Fire of London started during the day.		
The fire started in Pudding Lane.		
King Charles II designed a new city.		

2 marks

5 Put ticks in the table to show which statements are **true** and which statements are **false**. (Pages 6–7)

Statement	True	False
The man who discovered the fire was a baker.		
Oil and brandy were stored in warehouses.		
The wind was blowing from the west.		
London was rebuilt very quickly.		

2 marks

6 Tick to show where different building materials were used before the fire. (Pages 6–7)

	Lead	Wood	Stone
Houses in Pudding Lane			
Walls of St Paul's Cathedral			
Roof of St Paul's Cathedral			

1 mark

Total marks .... /9   How am I doing?

41

Preparing for Paper 2

Explaining Non-Fiction

> These questions are about *The Great Fire of London*.

1 What made the warehouses by the river catch fire? (Page 6)

_____

_____

1 mark

2 Why did the oil and brandy in the warehouses make the fire worse? (Page 6)

_____

1 mark

3 How did the strong east wind help the fire to spread? (Page 6)

_____

1 mark

4 How was the Mayor wrong about the fire? (Page 6)

_____

1 mark

Preparing for Paper 2

Explaining Non-Fiction

5 Why did the fire die down in the end? (Page 7)

_____

1 mark

6 Why was the whole of London not rebuilt according to Christopher Wren's plans? (Page 7)

_____

_____

1 mark

7 What was the problem with building houses out of wood? (Page 7)

_____

1 mark

8 What was special about the roof of the new St Paul's Cathedral? (Page 7)

_____

1 mark

Total marks ………… /8   How am I doing?

43

Preparing for Paper 2

Looking for Clues in Non-Fiction

These questions are about *The Great Fire of London*.

1 How do you think the hot, dry weather affected the fire? (Page 6)

_____

_____
◯ 1 mark

2 How might the *narrow, crammed* streets have made the fire worse? (Page 6)

_____

_____
◯ 1 mark

3 How do you know that King Charles II took the fire more seriously than the Mayor? (Page 6)

_____

_____
◯ 1 mark

4 Why is it surprising that St Paul's Cathedral was destroyed by the fire? (Page 6)

_____

_____
◯ 1 mark

Preparing for Paper 2

Looking for Clues in Non-Fiction

5 Do you think it is easy to melt lead? (Pages 6–7)

Give a reason for your answer.

_____

_____

_____

1 mark

6 Why do you think people were told to tidy their rubbish away when London had been rebuilt? (Page 7)

_____

_____

1 mark

7 Based on what you have read, what other type of building might Londoners have wanted to build out of brick or stone? (Page 7)

Give a reason for your answer.

_____

_____

1 mark

8 Why do you think the fire of 1666 was called the *Great* Fire of London? (Pages 6–7)

_____

_____

1 mark

Total marks ………… /8   How am I doing?

Preparing for Paper 2

Progress Test 2

These questions are about *The Monkey's Heart*.

1 **Find** and **copy one** word that shows that the monkey was afraid when the crocodile began to rock from side to side in the water. (Page 5)

_____

1 mark

2 The monkey says *What a shame*. (Page 5)

This means…

Tick one.

What a trick. ☐

What a mistake. ☐

What a mess. ☐

What a pity. ☐

1 mark

3 Does the monkey live on the same side of the river as the crocodiles? (Page 4)

Give a reason for your answer.

_____

_____

1 mark

4 Why does the crocodile believe the monkey when he says he has left his heart in a tree? (Page 5)

_____

1 mark

46

Preparing for Paper 2

Progress Test 2

5 Number the sentences from 1 to 4 to show the order they happened in the story. *(Pages 4–5)*

The first one has been done for you.

Tick one.

The crocodile tells the monkey they plan to eat him. ☐

The monkey says he needs to go back to get his heart. ☐

The monkey hops onto the crocodile's back. [1]

The monkey escapes into the trees. ☐

1 mark

These questions are about *The Great Fire of London*.

6 The Mayor of London was not *worried* about the fire. *(Page 6)*

This means that he was not…

Tick one.

nervous. ☐

concerned. ☐

afraid. ☐

angry. ☐

1 mark

47

Preparing for Paper 2

Progress Test 2

7 Why doesn't the King's plan to stop the fire work? (Page 6)

_____

_____
1 mark

8 **Find** and **copy one** word from paragraph 8 that means *told*. (Page 7)

_____
1 mark

9 King Charles did not have enough money to build all of the buildings designed by Christopher Wren. (Page 7)

Write the name of one of his buildings that King Charles *did* pay for.

_____
1 mark

10 Why do you think it took years to rebuild London? (Page 7)

_____

_____
1 mark

Total marks ………… /10   How am I doing?

48

Answers

The KS1 English Reading test assesses five elements of the national curriculum ('content domain references'). The references for these elements are shown below. They are included within the answers to show which element each question is assessing and to help you to track children's progress.

- **1a** use knowledge of vocabulary to understand texts
- **1b** identify and explain key parts of texts, including characters, events, titles and information
- **1c** identify and explain sequence(s) of events in texts
- **1d** make inferences from texts
- **1e** predict what might happen next in texts, based on what has been read already

Question	Requirement	Marks	Content domain ref.
\multicolumn{4}{c}{**Pages 4–5 Word Meanings in Poems**}
1	Everyone complained.	1	1a
2	gloomy.	1	1a
3	Timothy danced because he was happy.	1	1a
\multicolumn{4}{c}{**Pages 6–7 Finding Words in Poems**}
1	crawling	1	1a
2	silently	1	1a
3	drake	1	1a
4	respond	1	1a
\multicolumn{4}{c}{**Pages 8–9 Understanding Poetry**}
1	grey	1	1b
2	Near the end of the day.	1	1b
3	the camera	1	1b
4	the old drake	1	1b
\multicolumn{4}{c}{**Pages 10–11 Finding Information in Non-Fiction**}
1	In forests, deserts or boggy swamps	1	1b
2	Because nobody had wheels.	1	1b
3	<table><tr><td></td><td>People</td><td>Animals</td></tr><tr><td>carried heavy loads</td><td></td><td>✓</td></tr><tr><td>walked everywhere</td><td>✓</td><td></td></tr></table>	1	1b
4	a wild donkey	1	1b
5	Iraq	1	1b
6	Wooden planks (Accept 'wood' or 'planks')	1	1b
\multicolumn{4}{c}{**Pages 12–13 Explaining Non-Fiction**}
1	They used the rope to drag things along.	1	1b
2	The logs make the load roll along.	1	1b

49

Answers

3	wheels	1	1b
4	They were very heavy.	1	1b
5	To make the wheels lighter/less heavy.	1	1b
6	They gave a much smoother ride.	1	1b
Pages 14–15 Finding Information in Fiction			
1	In a field	1	1b
2	Heart-shaped	1	1b
3	He was afraid of the dark.	1	1b
4	Plop's mummy/Mrs Barn Owl	1	1b
5	Plop does not want to be a **night** bird. Plop wants to be a **day** bird.	1	1b
6	no	1	1b
Pages 16–17 Explaining Fiction			
1	Mrs Barn Owl wants to help Plop not to be afraid of the dark.	1	1b
2	Because he does not know about it.	1	1b
3	Any two of: silver; blue; grey; black	1	1b
4	Because he has never had his beak outside the nest-hole at night time/after dark.	1	1b
5	Down into the world (Accept 'outside the nest-hole'.)	1	1b
6	Now	1	1b
Page 18 Putting Events in Order			
1	1. Plop lived with his mummy and daddy. 2. Plop was fat and fluffy. 3. Plop had knackety knees. 4. Plop was afraid of the dark.	1	1c
2	1. Plop tells his mummy he is afraid of the dark. 2. Plop's mummy wants to help him not to be afraid. 3. Plop's mummy tells him he does not know enough about the dark. 4. Plop's mummy tells him to go down into the world.	1	1c
Pages 19 Predicting What Will Happen			
1	Plop will go down into the world during the day time.	1	1e
2	Acceptable points: Plop may feel nervous or scared because he is a very young owl and has not been down into the world before.	1	1e
Pages 20–23 Looking for Clues in Fiction			
1	Award 1 mark for one of the following: • The nest is high up in the tree. • Plop is worried about landing safely.	1	1d
2	He might fall over/he might hurt himself.	1	1d
3	He shut his eyes. He took a deep breath.	1	1d
4	Award 1 mark for one of the following: • He is moving very quickly and fireworks move quickly. • He is spinning around and Catherine-wheel fireworks spin round.	1	1d

Answers

5	He is disappointed because he loves fireworks/he thinks fireworks are exciting.	1	1d
6	The little boy loves fireworks AND/OR As soon as it gets dark they will light the fireworks.	1	1d
7	amazement	1	1a
8	The little boy loves fireworks so he feels that Plop is missing out on something fun because owls do not have fireworks.	1	1d
9	Because he laughs when Plop asks if you eat fireworks.	1	1d
10	whizz	1	1a
11	Because the owls live higher up in the tree than the squirrels so they may have a better view.	1	1d
12	He wants Plop to be able to see the fireworks.	1	1d
	**Pages 24–27 Progress Test 1**

1	a flower	1	1a
2	drooping	1	1a
3	(sat) by a stone	1	1b
4	the sun (to shine)	1	1b
5	Concrete	1	1b
6	No (he is retired).	1	1b
7	The balcony was filled with colourful flowers.	1	1a
8	(a thick coat of) spines	1	1b
9	They curl up in a ball with all their spines sticking out. (Children should identify both details.)	1	1b
10	(see table below)	2	1b

Sentence	True	False
Hedgehogs are black.		✓
Male and female hedgehogs look very different.		✓
Hedgehogs have long noses.	✓	
Baby hedgehogs are called hoglets.	✓	

11	It is true.	1	1b
12	20–30 cm (Accept either 20 cm or 30 cm)	1	1b
13	Because they are nocturnal.	1	1b
14	Five years	1	1b

Page 28 Word Meanings in Fiction

1	He lay in the sun.	1	1a
2	The crocodile was not very clever.	1	1a

Page 29 Finding Words in Fiction

1	complained	1	1a
2	yawned	1	1a
3	rushing	1	1a
4	plan	1	1a
5	jeered	1	1a

Answers

	Pages 30–31 Understanding Fiction		
1	mangoes	1	1b
2	He floats in the water.	1	1b
3	<table><tr><th>Sentence</th><th>True</th><th>False</th></tr><tr><td>The crocodile and his wife eat a lot of fish.</td><td>✓</td><td></td></tr><tr><td>The weather in the story is hot.</td><td>✓</td><td></td></tr><tr><td>The monkey was sitting in a fig tree.</td><td></td><td>✓</td></tr><tr><td>The crocodile tells the monkey a joke.</td><td></td><td>✓</td></tr></table>	2	1b
4	<table><tr><th>Sentence</th><th>True</th><th>False</th></tr><tr><td>The monkey agrees to go for dinner with the crocodiles.</td><td>✓</td><td></td></tr><tr><td>The monkey swims across the river.</td><td></td><td>✓</td></tr><tr><td>The monkey escapes into a tree.</td><td>✓</td><td></td></tr><tr><td>The monkey calls the crocodile 'fish-face'.</td><td></td><td>✓</td></tr></table>	2	1b
5	<table><tr><th>Trick</th><th>Animal</th></tr><tr><td>Pretends to be a friend but plans to eat him.</td><td>crocodile</td></tr><tr><td>Pretends he does not have his heart with him.</td><td>monkey</td></tr></table>	1	1b
6	in a fig tree	1	1b
	Pages 32–33 Explaining Fiction		
1	The crocodile says it is too hot to catch the monkey/be rushing around.	1	1b
2	Because his wife is angry and upset with him/says he doesn't love her enough.	1	1b
3	Its heart	1	1b
4	All afternoon	1	1b
5	They see him by the river often and want to get to know him better.	1	1b
6	On the crocodile's back	1	1b
7	On special occasions	1	1b
8	Because he is looking forward to eating the monkey's (sweet) heart.	1	1b
9	Because the monkey tells him he does not have his heart with him.	1	1b
10	Accept one from: • He stopped and looked back. • He laughed at the crocodile. • He called him a 'fish-brain'.	1	1b

52

Answers

	Page 34 Putting Events in Order		
1	1. The crocodile's wife says she is tired of eating fish. 2. The crocodile's wife asks him to catch the monkey. 3. The crocodile thinks of a plan to catch the monkey. 4. The crocodile swims across to the far riverbank.	1	1c
2	1. The warehouses caught fire. 2. King Charles II told people to pull down houses to try and stop the fire. 3. St Paul's Cathedral was destroyed. 4. Christopher Wren designed a new city.	1	1c
	Page 35 Predicting What Will Happen		
1	She will be very angry with the crocodile.	1	1e
2	1 mark for: The monkey will not trust a crocodile again. 1 mark for explanation: We know this because the monkey says 'so much for making friends with a crocodile' which suggests he will not make friends with a crocodile again. OR The monkey says "I'll never trust you again!".	2	1e
	Pages 36–37 Looking for Clues in Fiction		
1	Because she was angry that he did not want to catch the monkey.	1	1d
2	Because he wanted to seem friendly so that the monkey will trust him.	1	1d
3	sighed	1	1a
4	The monkey is not afraid because he has a plan to escape from the crocodile. OR The monkey is afraid because he might be eaten, but he is hiding his fear because he wants to trick the crocodile and get away. (Either answer is acceptable, provided an appropriate reason is given.)	1	1d
5	Because the crocodile told the monkey about the plan before they reached the other side of the river, which gave the monkey time to think of a way to escape. OR The monkey is too clever/cleverer than the crocodile.	1	1d
6	Because he knows the crocodile is not very clever and will take him back to the riverbank to collect the heart, giving him a chance to escape. OR He knows crocodiles can't climb trees so he can escape.	1	1d
7	Because he thinks the crocodile is silly/stupid for being tricked so easily. OR 'fish-brain' implies a small brain.	1	1d
8	No, because the monkey accepts the crocodile's offer to ride on his back to cross the river. AND/OR He is alarmed when the crocodile begins to rock from side to side, which suggests he would not be able to swim if he fell off.	1	1d
	Page 38 Word Meanings in Non-Fiction		
1	quickly.	1	1a
2	powerful.	1	1a
	Page 39 Finding Words in Non-Fiction		
1	narrow	1	1a
2	crammed	1	1a
3	goods	1	1a
4	streets	1	1a
5	Finally	1	1a

Answers

Pages 40–41 Understanding Non-Fiction

1	Tuesday				1	1b
2	King Charles II				1	1b

3.

	Before the Fire	After the Fire
Rubbish in the streets	✓	
New buildings built of brick or stone		✓
Houses made of wood	✓	
Fire brigades set up		✓

2 marks | 1b

4.

Statement	True	False
The summer of 1666 was hot in London.	✓	
The Great Fire of London started during the day.		✓
The fire started in Pudding Lane.	✓	
King Charles II designed a new city.		✓

2 marks | 1b

5.

Statement	True	False
The man who discovered the fire was a baker.	✓	
Oil and brandy were stored in warehouses.	✓	
The wind was blowing from the west.		✓
London was rebuilt very quickly.		✓

2 marks | 1b

6.

	Lead	Wood	Stone
Houses in Pudding Lane		✓	
Walls of St Paul's Cathedral			✓
Roof of St Paul's Cathedral	✓		

1 mark | 1b

Pages 42–43 Explaining Non-Fiction

1	Sparks landed on them. OR They were full of flammable goods like oil and brandy.	1	1b
2	Because they are flammable/burn easily.	1	1b
3	It fanned the flames.	1	1b
4	He thought it would be easy to put out/would be out by morning.	1	1b
5	The wind changed direction.	1	1b
6	There was not enough money/King Charles could not afford to build everything in the plan.	1	1b
7	They burnt easily.	1	1b
8	It was domed.	1	1b

Answers

	Pages 44–45 Looking for Clues in Non-Fiction		
1	It would have made the fire worse because things that are dry burn more easily.	1	1d
2	The fire would have spread easily from house to house because they were close together.	1	1d
3	Because the Mayor thought the fire would be easy to put out, but the King actually tried to put it out/had a plan.	1	1d
4	Because it was built of stone and stone cannot burn.	1	1d
5	No, because the text says that it melted because the flames were 'so fierce', suggesting that only a very hot fire would melt lead.	1	1d
6	So that if there was another fire, burning rubbish would not help the fire to spread from building to building.	1	1d
7	Warehouses, because they are used to store goods that are flammable/burn easily, like oil and brandy, so they should be built from stone. OR Their own houses, so they would feel safe.	1	1d
8	The word 'Great' suggests that the fire was very large. Children may also infer that the fire was memorable because of its size.	1	1d
	Pages 46–48 Progress Test 2		
1	alarm	1	1a
2	What a pity.	1	1a
3	No, because the monkey crosses the river on the crocodile's back to get from his home to the crocodiles' home. OR It says the crocodile swam over to the 'far riverbank', (i.e. a different side). OR It says '"We live on the other side," said the crocodile'.	1	1d
4	Because he is not very clever.	1	1d
5	1. The monkey hops onto the crocodile's back. 2. The crocodile tells the monkey they plan to eat him. 3. The monkey says he needs to go back to get his heart. 4. The monkey escapes into the trees.	1	1c
6	concerned.	1	1a
7	Because the flames were too big and they jumped across the gap left by pulling down the houses.	1	1b
8	instructed	1	1a
9	St Paul's Cathedral	1	1b
10	Accept any from: 1. Many buildings needed to be rebuilt. 2. It took longer to build buildings from stone than wood. 3. Money had to be provided/found for the building work, which took time.	1	1d

Progress Test Charts

Progress Test 1

Q	Topic	✓ or ✗	See page
1	Word Meanings in Poems		4
2	Finding Words in Poems		6
3	Understanding Poetry		8
4	Understanding Poetry		8
5	Finding Information in Fiction		14
6	Finding Information in Fiction		14
7	Explaining Fiction		16
8	Finding Information in Non-Fiction		10
9	Finding Information in Non-Fiction		10
10	Finding Information in Non-Fiction		10
11	Explaining Non-Fiction		12
12	Explaining Non-Fiction		12
13	Explaining Non-Fiction		12
14	Finding Information in Non-Fiction		10

Progress Test 2

Q	Topic	✓ or ✗	See page
1	Finding Words in Fiction		29
2	Word Meanings in Fiction		28
3	Looking for Clues in Fiction		36
4	Looking for Clues in Fiction		36
5	Putting Events in Order		34
6	Word Meanings in Non-Fiction		38
7	Finding Information in Non-Fiction		10
8	Finding Words in Non-Fiction		39
9	Finding Information in Non-Fiction		10
10	Looking for Clues in Non-Fiction		44

What am I doing well in?

_____

_____

_____

What do I need to improve?

_____

_____

_____

ACKNOWLEDGEMENTS

The author and publisher are grateful to the copyright holders for permission to use quoted materials and images.
P.4, 6, 8 'When Daddy Fell into the Pond' by Alfred Noyes. The Society of Authors as the Literary Representative of the Estate of Alfred Noyes; P.10, 11, 12, 13 Reproduced from The Story of Inventions (by Anna Claybourne) by permission of Usborne Publishing, 83-85 Saffron Hill, London EC1N 8RT, UK. www.usborne.com. Copyright © 2012 Usborne Publishing Ltd; P.14, 15, 16, 17, 20, 21, 22, 23 From The Owl Who Was Afraid of the Dark by Jill Tomlinson. Text copyright © 1968 Jill Tomlinson. Published by Egmont UK Ltd and used with permission; P.25 From Esio Trot by Roald Dahl. Reproduced by kind permission of Jonathan Cape Ltd and Penguin Books Ltd; P.26, 27 From HEDGEHOGS by Sally Morgan, first published in the UK by Franklin Watts, an imprint of Hachette Children's Books, Carmelite House, 50 Victoria Embankment, London, EC4Y 0DZ; P.2-5 (of Reading Booklet) Reproduced from Stories from India (by Anna Milbourne) by permission of Usborne Publishing, 83-85 Saffron Hill, London EC1N 8RT, UK. www.usborne.com. Copyright © 2009 Usborne Publishing Ltd
P.4, 6, 8, 14–17, 20–23 Illustrations by Nigel Lancashire at Rose & Thorn Creative Services Ltd.
All other illustrations and images © Shutterstock.com
Every effort has been made to trace copyright holders and obtain their permission for the use of copyright material. The author and publisher will gladly receive information enabling them to rectify any error or omission in subsequent editions. All facts are correct at time of going to press.

Published by Collins
An imprint of HarperCollinsPublishers
1 London Bridge Street
London SE1 9GF

© HarperCollinsPublishers Limited 2017
ISBN 9780008253127
First published 2017
10 9 8 7 6 5 4 3 2 1

All rights reserved. No part of this publication may be reproduced, stored in a retrieval system, or transmitted, in any form or by any means, electronic, mechanical, photocopying, recording or otherwise, without the prior permission of Collins.
British Library Cataloguing in Publication Data.
A CIP record of this book is available from the British Library.
Author: Alison Head
Commissioning Editor: Michelle l'Anson
Editors/Project Managers: Rebecca Skinner and Katie Galloway
Cover and Inside Concept Design: Paul Oates
Text Design and Layout: Contentra Technologies
Production: Natalia Rebow
Printed and bound in China by RR Donnelley APS